NATIONAL
GEOGRA

T0303079

Alexander Graham Bell
and the Telephone

Anita Garmon

Contents

Alexander Graham Bell grew up in a family that had a special interest in teaching deaf people to speak. Both his father and his grandfather were speech teachers. Alexander became a teacher of the deaf, too.

Alexander Graham Bell was also an inventor. He taught during the day and experimented at night. His most famous invention became the telephone. It forever changed the way people communicated.

Alexander Graham Bell became famous for his invention of the telephone.

Chapter 1

The Young Bell

A lexander Graham Bell was born on March 3, 1847, in Edinburgh, Scotland. He was the second of three sons. Alexander was named for his grandfather, Alexander Bell. He later gave himself a middle name, Graham.

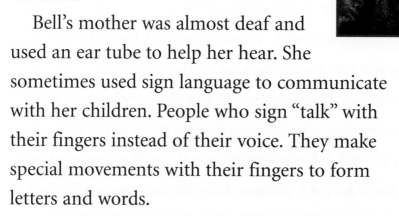

Bell's mother was almost deaf and used an ear tube to help her hear. She sometimes used sign language to communicate with her children. People who sign "talk" with their fingers instead of their voice. They make special movements with their fingers to form letters and words.

Even though she had a hearing problem, Bell's mother was a fine musician. She put her ear tube on the soundboard of the piano. This way she could "hear" the notes by feeling the vibrations the piano made.

To help her to hear, Alexander Graham Bell's mother used an ear tube.

Think about this. If you cannot hear, then how can you speak? You wouldn't know how to make sounds. Bell's father had invented a way to teach deaf people to speak. It was called "Visible Speech." He created pictures that showed how you use your tongue and lips to make certain sounds. These pictures showed deaf people how to pronounce words they could not hear.

Even as a young boy, Bell was interested in the human voice. He and his brother built a speaking machine. The machine could say "Mama."

The pictures used in "Visible Speech" showed deaf people how to pronounce words without hearing them.

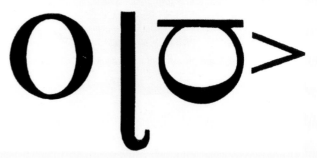

Alexander Bell started inventing when he was 11. His father's friend, a mill-owner, invited him to create something useful. And he did. Bell created a tool to take the husks, or outer shells, off wheat kernels. He did not become rich or famous from his first invention. But he learned that he could invent things.

Alexander Graham Bell began inventing things when he was a child. He was 14 when this photo was taken.

Young Bell may have been very smart, but he was not a good student. He had no interest in Greek or Latin, two important subjects taught at school. Instead, he wanted to study plants and animals. Like his mother, he loved music and took piano lessons.

After Bell graduated from high school, his father sent him to live and study with his grandfather in London. Bell's grandfather was a speech expert. He taught people how to be better speakers. At that time, people had to talk loudly and clearly to be heard. There were no microphones or public address systems as there are today.

Bell enjoyed living with his grandfather. His grandfather let Bell make his own decisions. Young Bell became a more serious student. He learned a lot about the human voice and how it works. He decided that he would become a teacher like his grandfather and father.

Alexander Graham Bell wanted to become a teacher like his father and grandfather.

Chapter 2

Teaching Speech

B ell applied for a job as a teacher of speech and music in Scotland. Although he was only 16 years old, he got the job. Some of his students were older than he was. While teaching, Bell studied the voice. He also experimented with sound.

Bell's family moved to London. There, his father taught his system of "Visible Speech." Bell joined his family in London. He began teaching his father's system to children with hearing and speech problems. He continued to study human speech and to test his ideas on sound and electricity. Bell was sure that the human voice could travel through electrical wires.

But tragedy struck the Bell family. Bell's two brothers died. His father feared that Alexander would become ill and die, too. So, Bell's father moved the family to Canada. He thought Canada was a healthier place to live. Bell was 23 years old.

Alexander Graham Bell began teaching speech as a young man.

Bell wanted to live his own life. A year after moving to Canada, he moved to Boston. A young woman, Sarah Fuller, had started a school in Boston using his father's speech system. Bell went there to teach.

Bell soon became known as a successful teacher. Unlike many teachers at the time, he was patient with his students. He showed them how the voice worked. He taught them to use their fingers to feel their speech. He showed them how to move their lips and tongue to make sounds. Instead of punishing his students, he helped them. Bell had great success with many of his students.

The more Bell worked with his students, the more certain he became that he could send voice messages over electrical wires. So Bell taught during the day and experimented at night.

Alexander Graham Bell taught speech at the Boston School for the Deaf.

Chapter 3

Racing to Be First

Bell became a professor at a university in Boston. He also gave private lessons. One of his students was Mabel Hubbard. She had become deaf at the age of five from a disease called scarlet fever. Bell fell in love with her. They would marry two years later. Her father, Gardiner Hubbard, was a successful businessman and lawyer.

Mabel Hubbard was a deaf student taught by Alexander Graham Bell.

Bell told Gardiner Hubbard and Thomas Sanders, the father of another of Bell's students, about his experiments and ideas. The two men agreed to give Bell money to work full time on his ideas. This was important because other inventors were also working on ideas like Bell's. The first one to invent a machine to send sound over an electric wire would become rich.

Bell hired an assistant. Bell's assistant, Thomas Watson, knew a lot about electricity. They made a good team.

Thomas Watson helped Alexander Graham Bell invent the telephone.

Bell learned that one other inventor was racing to complete what would become the telephone. Elisha Gray worked hard on his invention, too. It was a race to the U.S. Patent Office.

A patent is a paper from the government that gives the holder certain rights. For a set period of time, only the holder of the patent can sell, use, or make a certain invention. Whoever got the patent first would "own" the invention of the telephone.

Bell worked on his patent application for months. Wanting to be the first to file for the patent, Hubbard filed Bell's unfinished application on February 14, 1876. Just two hours later, Gray applied for a patent as well. Bell was awarded the patent. He had won the race by just two hours!

Bell kept detailed records of his work. This drawing shows one of his early ideas for the telephone.

Wednesday April 5th

Figure I

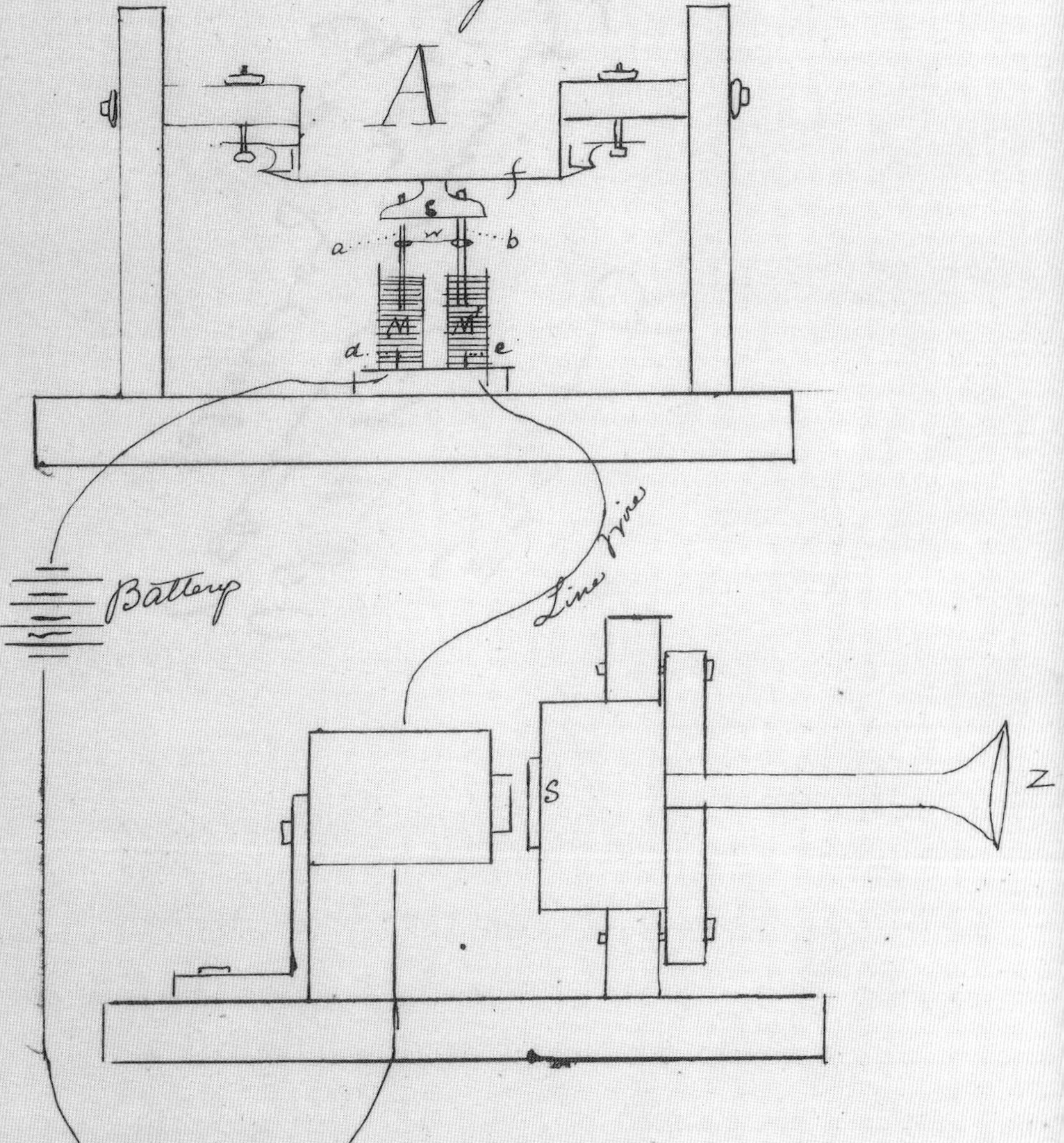
A
f
S
w
a
b
M
M'
d
e
Line Wire
Battery
S
Z

1. Apparatus arranged as in Fig 1. 16 a
cork attached to a membrane f. The co

Chapter 4

Making the Telephone

N ow Bell had to actually make a telephone that worked. He and Watson continued to test different models. Finally, on March 10, 1876, Bell sent his voice over the wires!

Bell was in one room and Watson was in a different one. Bell said, "Mr. Watson, come here, I want to see you!" Watson rushed in saying that he had heard Bell's voice! Bell's voice was hard to hear, but it still seemed like a miracle.

Bell and Watson worked to make the sound of the human voice clearer and easier to understand. At first, speech traveled only one way. Bell worked on his telephone and put a transmitter and receiver at both ends of the phone. Then people could have two-way conversations, just like we can today.

Now Bell had to make people think that the telephone was a useful invention. Some people thought it was more like a toy.

This is a model of the transmitter that Bell first used to send his voice over the wires.

In 1876, there was a big fair in Philadelphia. Many inventors showed their inventions. Scientists and businessmen visited the fair. Bell decided to show his invention, too. Once people heard Bell's voice come over the wire, the telephone became the hit of the fair. Newspapers carried stories about this strange, new invention.

Bell, with Watson, Hubbard, and Sanders, formed the Bell Telephone Company. Bell left the selling and making of the telephone to his partners. He went off to London with his new wife, Mabel.

This drawing shows Alexander Graham Bell demonstrating his telephone.

While Bell was in London, the telephone became famous. People asked Bell to show them how it worked. Queen Victoria, the ruler of England, asked Bell to show her how the telephone worked. She loved it. She demanded that phones be put in her palace. By 1880, the telephone had become one of the most famous and popular inventions of all time.

Alexander Graham Bell made the first telephone call from New York to Chicago.

Chapter 5

Other Inventions

Alexander Graham Bell's invention made him a rich man. He decided that he did not want to be involved in business. He just wanted to be an inventor. So Bell left the Telephone Company. He was only 32 years old.

Bell continued to invent and experiment. He built a lab that he worked in all year. He loved to design and fly kites. Bell and his team built a plane in 1908 that won an award. He also built a boat that had skis. That boat is now known as a hydrofoil.

Alexander Graham Bell designed many kites.

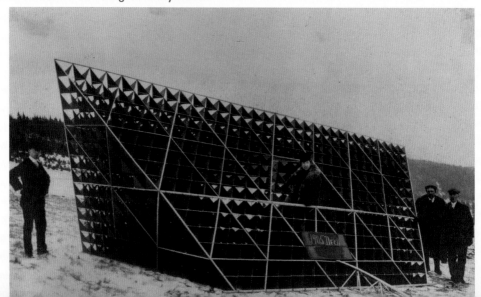

Bell invented one machine in response to a sad event. Bell's son had died hours after being born because he had trouble breathing. Bell decided to make an invention to help people to breathe. He made a machine that pumped air in and out of the lungs. This machine became known as the "iron lung." It saved the lives of thousands of people and is still being used today.

Bell received many awards for his work. People all over the world knew and admired him. When Bell died, in 1922 at age 75, all the telephones in the United States were quiet for one minute. People did this to honor Bell.

This bank note honors Alexander Graham Bell and the invention of the telephone.